Table of Conten

GW00457208

Chapter 1: Introduction

The Concept of a Modern Single-Style Martial Arts School

In the ever-evolving landscape of martial arts, diversity has often been seen as the key to a successful school. Many establishments boast a variety of styles, from Karate to Jiu-Jitsu, Taekwondo to Kung Fu, hoping to attract a broader audience. However, the tide is shifting towards specialization, and the concept of a modern single-style martial arts school is gaining traction. This approach can bring numerous advantages, particularly in terms of focused training, streamlined progression, and deep mastery - all of which can lead to higher student satisfaction and retention.

A single-style martial arts school places its bets on one martial art system. Instead of being a jack-of-all-trades, it aspires to be a master of one. This focused approach aligns with the ancient philosophy of martial arts, which prizes depth of knowledge and mastery of technique above all. It provides students with the opportunity to immerse themselves fully in a single discipline, learning its nuances and intricacies in a way that would be impossible in a multi-style school.

In this school model, the emphasis is on delivering a comprehensive, progressive, and engaging program that caters to different age groups and experience levels. Whether it's the Lil Dragons for 5 to 7-year-olds, Juniors for 8 to 12-year-olds, advanced Juniors, or Teens and Adult programs, the core martial art remains the same. The difference lies in the teaching methods, intensity, and specific techniques taught, which are carefully tailored to the learning capabilities and objectives of each age group or experience level.

The single-style martial arts school model presents unique marketing opportunities, allowing the school to position itself as a specialist in the chosen martial art. This positioning can be highly attractive to prospective students who are looking for an authentic and in-depth learning experience.

Moreover, this model brings a sense of predictability and orderliness to the school's operations. With classes and instructors dedicated to a specific style, scheduling becomes easier. By assigning students to specific time bands based on their age and level, the school can ensure that each class caters to a particular group of students and is thus as effective and engaging as possible.

Lastly, the financial aspects of running a single-style martial arts school can be more straightforward to manage. With a clear understanding of the number of students and classes, the revenue potential can be accurately calculated. Pricing strategies can be developed to reflect the value delivered in each class, and instructor compensation can be aligned with class revenue, fostering a sense of ownership and commitment among the staff.

This book will delve into the intricacies of running a modern single-style martial arts school, from choosing the style and structuring the programs, to managing the schedule, staff, and finances. It will provide insights into the potential challenges and how to navigate them, as well as the opportunities that this model presents. Whether you're an experienced martial arts school owner looking to revamp your establishment or a new entrant planning to set up a school, this book will equip you with the knowledge and tools to succeed in your endeavor.

Scope of the Book

This book aims to provide a comprehensive guide to operating a single-style martial arts school successfully. It offers practical insights and strategies that cover a broad spectrum of the business aspects, from defining the core program and structuring classes to marketing the school and managing its financial health.

The following areas will be thoroughly discussed:

- **Choosing and Implementing Your Martial Arts Program:** We delve into the benefits of a single-style system and provide guidance on implementing it. We'll explore the concepts of deep mastery, focused training, and streamlined progression to ensure students get the most out of the chosen martial arts style.

- **Developing Effective Training Programs:** Detailed breakdowns of youth, adult, and advanced programs will be covered. We'll provide insights into setting up schedules, pricing structures, and how to cater to different age groups and experience levels within the chosen style.

- **Staffing and Instructor Management:** A significant portion of the book will be dedicated to building a strong team. We'll cover instructor roles, hiring practices, performance-based compensation, and strategies to enhance engagement and professional development among staff members.

- **Marketing Your School:** This section will outline how to effectively market your specialized martial arts school, including identifying the unique selling propositions of a single-style school and how to communicate this to your target audience.

- **Financial Management:** We'll take a deep dive into the financial aspects of running a martial arts school. This includes revenue potential, expense breakdown, profit margin analysis, and strategies for balancing costs with income to ensure financial success.

- **Curriculum Design:** The book will conclude with a focus on the design and implementation of a rotating curriculum. We'll explore how this can offer scalability, continuity, and structured learning that benefits both the students and the school.

Throughout the book, real-life examples and practical advice will be presented to make the process of running a single-style martial arts school as smooth as possible. We aim to equip you with a comprehensive understanding of this unique model, empowering you to make informed decisions and strategically guide your school towards success.

Chapter 2:The Backbone.

Your Martial Arts Program

Choosing the Single Style for Your School
Deciding which martial arts style to offer at your school is perhaps the most critical decision you will make as a school owner. This choice will shape not only the training programs and curriculum but also the overall culture and identity of your school. It will impact your marketing strategies, your target audience, and the instructors you hire. Here are some key considerations when choosing the single style for your school:

1. Personal Mastery and Passion: The first rule of opening a martial arts school is to teach what you know and love. Your personal passion and mastery of the style will reflect in the quality of training and the enthusiasm you bring to the classes. If you are not an expert, consider partnering with someone who is, or invest time and resources into mastering the style before you start teaching it. Your credibility as an instructor is vital to the success of your school.

2. Market Demand: It's important to conduct a thorough market analysis to understand what styles are already being offered in your area and whether there is a demand for the style you plan to teach. Consider conducting surveys or informal interviews with people in your community to gauge interest. However, don't be discouraged if the style you're considering isn't popular yet. Part of your role will be to educate your community about its benefits.

3. Compatibility with Target Demographics: Different martial arts styles appeal to different age groups and demographics. For instance, styles that involve high-intensity physical conditioning and sparring might be more popular with younger students, while styles that emphasize mindfulness, discipline, and gradual progression might attract a more diverse age range.

4. Values and Philosophy: Each martial art comes with its own set of values and philosophical underpinnings. Some styles are more competitive, others emphasize self-defense, while some are more about personal growth and discipline. Choose a style that aligns with your personal values and the impact you want to make in your students' lives.

5. Practicality: Finally, consider practical factors such as the space required for training, necessary equipment, and the safety aspects of the style. Some styles might require larger training areas or specific training equipment, which can add to your start-up and operational costs. Choosing a single style for your martial arts school is not a decision to be taken lightly. It's important to take the time to evaluate your options and consider the short and long-term implications of your choice. Remember, the style you choose will become the heart and soul of your school, setting the tone for everything you do.

Deep Mastery

In the context of a martial arts school, deep mastery goes beyond acquiring a set of techniques; it refers to a profound understanding and embodiment of the chosen martial arts system, extending to its strategies, philosophies, traditions, and even its historical and cultural contexts.

Understanding of Techniques

The journey to deep mastery begins with the comprehensive learning and understanding of techniques. By focusing on a single martial arts system, students have the opportunity to learn every technique in depth, understanding not only how to execute them, but also when and why to use them. This in-depth understanding fosters a more intuitive application of techniques in different scenarios, enhancing students' performance during sparring or real-world applications.

Strategic Application

Deep mastery involves the development of strategic thinking. Students must understand the underlying principles that guide the application of techniques in various situations. This is where the knowledge of a single martial arts system becomes more than a sum of its parts. The principles learnt can help students adapt their techniques to different opponents and scenarios, fostering a strategic mindset that can be a game-changer in martial arts engagements.

Philosophical and Cultural Appreciation

Every martial arts system is deeply rooted in specific philosophical and cultural contexts. For instance, Brazilian Jiu-Jitsu has strong links to concepts of resilience, patience, and respect, whereas Krav Maga emphasizes practicality, adaptability, and determination. A deep mastery of a martial art involves an understanding and appreciation of these underlying philosophies, adding a depth of meaning to the physical practice.

Continuous Refinement

Deep mastery is not a destination but a journey of continuous learning and refinement. Even when a technique is well understood and can be effectively applied, there is always room for refinement and improvement. This iterative process of learning, practicing, refining, and relearning is what leads to deep mastery.

Transmission of Knowledge

Finally, deep mastery in a martial arts school setting involves the ability to transmit this knowledge effectively to students of different ages and skill levels. Instructors play a critical role in this process, as they not only need to have a deep understanding of the martial arts system themselves but must also be able to guide students on their path to mastery. By focusing on a single martial arts system, your school can foster this deep mastery among both instructors and students, creating a rich, meaningful, and rewarding martial arts learning environment.

Focused Training

Focused training is a key component of a single-system martial arts school. In such a setting, every class, drill, and exercise has a specific purpose aimed at enhancing the understanding and proficiency in the chosen martial art. The intensity and complexity of training sessions can be tailored accurately to fit the martial art's unique characteristics and requirements, allowing students to gradually build their skills and knowledge within the chosen system.

With a focus on a singular system, the students' training journey becomes a streamlined process of consistent and focused practice. Each technique is taught with an emphasis on its place within the larger system, creating an interconnected web of knowledge and skills that each student can navigate with increasing competence. This focus allows students to better understand the strategic underpinnings of their chosen martial art, as every technique learned is not an isolated skill but a piece of a bigger picture. Furthermore, the focused training approach in a single-system school facilitates a deeper instructor-student connection. As instructors are fully immersed in the system they teach, they can share their deep insights and experiences, closely monitor each student's progress, and provide targeted guidance. This close attention to individual progress can further enhance the effectiveness of training, creating a dynamic and engaging learning environment for all students.

In essence, focused training in a single-system martial arts school is a holistic, immersive, and highly personalized approach to martial arts education. It allows students to delve deep into their practice, fostering a profound understanding and mastery that can only be achieved through dedicated and focused training.

- Streamlined Progression Path

A streamlined progression path is an essential characteristic of a single-system martial arts school. It provides clarity and motivation for students, allowing them to understand where they are in their martial arts journey and what they need to do to reach the next level.

In a school focused on a single martial arts system, the progression path is directly aligned with the unique structure and philosophy of the system. It's meticulously designed to guide students from the basics to more advanced techniques and strategies. As students progress, they build upon their existing knowledge base, continually expanding their skillset within the context of the chosen martial art.

This structured approach provides clear milestones for students. These milestones can be formal, like belt rankings or achievement badges, or informal, like mastering a complex technique or achieving a personal best in a fitness test. These milestones serve to motivate students, giving them tangible goals to aim for and a sense of accomplishment when they are achieved.

Furthermore, a streamlined progression path provides a sense of transparency and fairness in the school. Students know what is expected of them at each level and what they need to achieve to progress. This clarity can enhance motivation and commitment, as students can see the results of their hard work and dedication. Importantly, this streamlined progression path is not rigid but adaptable to each student's pace. While the path is clear, students can progress at their own pace, ensuring that they fully understand and master each level before moving on to the next. This flexibility caters to individual learning styles and paces, ensuring each student feels challenged but not overwhelmed.

Ultimately, a streamlined progression path provides a clear roadmap for students' martial arts journey, fostering motivation, commitment, and a deep sense of achievement. It ensures that every student, regardless of their skill level or experience, knows where they are going and how to get there.

Chapter 3:Understanding Your Students

- <u>Segmenting by Age Group: An Overview of the Youth Programs</u>

Understanding the specific needs and abilities of different age groups is key to designing successful youth programs in your martial arts school. Here, we'll break down the youth segment into three distinct age groups: Lil Dragons (5-7 years old), Juniors (8-12 years old), and Advanced Juniors or BBT (Black Belt Training).

<u>Lil Dragons (5-7 years old):</u>
This age group is at the beginner stage, where the focus is on foundational skills, building confidence, and instilling a love for the martial art. The classes for Lil Dragons are structured as 30-minute sessions, which accommodate the shorter attention spans typical of this age group. While the sessions are designed to be fun and engaging, they are also structured to introduce basic martial arts techniques

and the discipline needed for more advanced training.

Based on the pricing structure outlined, each Lil Dragon class with full capacity can generate $2,800 per month. The classes are offered twice a week, which keeps the training consistent but not overwhelming for the children.

Juniors (8-12 years old):

At this age, children have developed better coordination, focus, and are able to handle more complex techniques. The Junior program classes are extended to 45 minutes and designed to cater to up to 20 students per class. The curriculum is designed to be more challenging than the Lil Dragons program, with a stronger focus on skill development, self-discipline, and respect for the martial art and others. The potential monthly income from each Junior class, at full capacity, is $4,000. The increased income reflects the higher value offered in this program, as students are learning more advanced techniques and dedicating more time to their training.

Advanced Juniors/BBT:

This program is designed for Juniors who show an exceptional commitment to their training and are ready for more advanced techniques. The curriculum continues to build on the skills acquired in the Junior program, but with a stronger emphasis on mastery, leadership skills, and preparing for black belt level training. The Advanced Juniors program also runs 45-minute classes and can accommodate up to 30 students, potentially generating $6,000 per month.

Segmenting your youth program into these age-specific classes allows you to provide more focused and appropriate training for each stage of development. Moreover, it also makes it easier for parents to understand the progression path and the value offered at each stage. This thoughtful segmentation strategy can play a key role in the financial success of your martial arts school.

- ## Segmenting by Experience Level: An Overview of the Adult Programs

In designing a martial arts school, it is critical to account for the wide range of experience and fitness levels among adults. The process of segmenting the adult programs by experience level ensures that each student receives appropriate and beneficial training, fostering both progression and satisfaction.

Here, the adult programs are classified into two primary categories: All Levels and Advanced. This division caters to the needs of beginners, intermediates, and advanced students alike. The flexibility of these categories accommodates students' evolution, offering clear progression paths within the school.

Adults: All Levels

This category embraces a spectrum of experience levels, from absolute beginners to those with a moderate level of expertise. In this program, the curriculum is designed to provide a comprehensive introduction to the martial art style, highlighting key techniques, stances, and movements. It's also intended to foster foundational physical fitness, flexibility, and coordination.

The program provides options for students to train once, twice, or unlimited times a week, with prices ranging from $150 to $250 per month. This flexibility accommodates a range of commitment levels and budgets, making the martial arts more accessible to a broader audience.

At full capacity, the All Levels program, accounting for most students on a twice-a-week training schedule, has a monthly revenue potential ranging from $12,000 to $16,000.

Advanced Adults

The Advanced program is designed for students who have demonstrated a solid understanding of the fundamental techniques and are ready to explore more complex aspects of the martial art. These classes provide a deeper dive into the style, with increased focus on strategy, precision, and the philosophy underlying the martial art.

Students in the Advanced program are typically those committed to long-term progression and mastery. The pricing for the Advanced program follows the same structure as the All Levels program.

As students advance in their training, they may feel an increased sense of commitment to the school, further driving revenue stability.

By offering programs tailored to different experience levels, your martial arts school can accommodate a wider range of students. This not only broadens your market appeal but also enhances student satisfaction and retention, contributing significantly to your school's overall success.

- Catering to Different Levels: The Streamlined Progression Path

A crucial aspect of managing a modern single-style martial arts school is designing a clear, streamlined progression path for students. This path serves as a roadmap for students, guiding them from beginner to advanced levels, building their proficiency, and deepening their commitment to the martial art. Here's how a streamlined progression path can be instrumental in successfully catering to different levels of students.

Transparent and Achievable Goals

A well-designed progression path offers transparent and achievable goals that students can aspire to reach. Each milestone, whether it's mastering a complex move, earning a new belt, or advancing to a higher level class, serves as a motivation. This drives students to consistently improve and dedicate more time and effort to their training.

Recognition of Achievement

Progression in martial arts is often marked by different colored belts or ranking systems. These symbols of achievement are crucial for student morale and motivation. They provide visible recognition of the students' hard work and dedication and affirm their progress. A streamlined progression path helps ensure these recognitions are distributed in a fair, timely, and systematic manner.

Increasing Complexity and Challenge

As students progress, the challenges they face in their training should correspondingly increase. This not only ensures their continued learning and skill improvement, but also keeps them engaged and interested in the martial art. A well-defined progression path helps manage this process by outlining when and how new techniques and concepts are introduced.

Tailored Training

Students at different stages of their martial arts journey have distinct needs and abilities. A beginner might need more focus on conditioning and basic techniques, while an advanced student might benefit from deep dives into strategy and philosophy. A streamlined progression path ensures that the training is appropriately tailored to each level, enhancing the value and effectiveness of each class.

In sum, a streamlined progression path provides structure and motivation for students, ensuring they are continually challenged and rewarded for their hard work. It serves as a roadmap for their martial arts journey, enhancing their experience and, in turn, contributing to the school's success.

Chapter 4:Scheduling for Success

- ## Designing an Effective Schedule
An effective schedule is the lifeblood of a martial arts school. It determines when your doors open, when classes are held, and who is teaching. A well-designed schedule is an efficient one – it makes optimal use of your resources, facilitates smooth operations, and, most importantly, serves the needs of your students. In this chapter, we delve into the principles of designing an effective schedule for a modern single-style martial arts school.

Understanding Your Students
The first step in designing an effective schedule is understanding who your students are and what their needs might be. Consider factors such as school hours for children, typical work hours for adults, and preferred times for classes. Some students might prefer early morning workouts, while others might opt for evening classes. Offering a range of class

times can help accommodate these diverse needs.

Maximizing Facility Use
The schedule should also take into consideration the capacity and layout of your facility. In the case of our one-floor school, each class is carefully slotted to cater to a specific group of students. This ensures efficient use of the available space and avoids overlaps that could lead to congestion or confusion.

Streamlining Class Sequences
The sequence of classes in the schedule is another key consideration. Grouping classes for similar age groups or levels together can help to simplify transitions and enhance focus. For example, in the provided schedule, Lil Dragons and Juniors are grouped together on Monday and Wednesday, while adult classes are grouped on Tuesday and Thursday. This allows instructors to adjust their teaching style and methods to cater to the specific group in a continuous manner, enhancing the effectiveness of each class.

Balancing Instructor Availability and Expertise

The schedule also needs to account for instructor availability and areas of expertise. For instance, if you have an instructor who excels at teaching beginners, schedule them for the All Levels classes. Performance-based compensation, as discussed in Chapter 3, can also be an effective tool to ensure instructors are motivated to teach their assigned classes well.

Incorporating Rest and Recovery

Lastly, the schedule should also provide ample time for rest and recovery, both for students and instructors. Avoid scheduling back-to-back intense classes and ensure that there is enough time between classes for facility cleaning and maintenance.

In conclusion, an effective schedule is a delicate balance of numerous factors. It requires a deep understanding of your students, careful resource allocation, and meticulous planning. However, the result is well worth the effort - a smoothly running school that provides high-quality training to satisfied students.

- Assigning Students to Specific Time Bands

One of the cornerstones of a successful single-style martial arts school is the strategic assignment of students to specific time bands. This systematic approach offers numerous benefits, both for the students and for the school's operations.

Assigning students to specific time bands creates a consistent and predictable class environment. The students in each band are likely to be at a similar level, either in terms of age or experience, which allows the instructor to tailor the class to their needs more effectively. For example, a class of Juniors (8-12 years old) at 4:15pm on Monday and Wednesday would focus on different techniques and aspects of the martial art compared to a class of Advanced Juniors (BBT) at 5:15pm on Tuesday and Thursday.

By keeping students within specific time bands, instructors can better track the progress of their students. They can observe the development of each student over time, identifying strengths to be celebrated and weaknesses to be addressed.

This personalized attention not only enhances the quality of instruction but also strengthens the bond between the students and the instructor.

From an operational perspective, this system facilitates better resource planning and financial management. Knowing the number of students in each band and their monthly fees allows the school to calculate the income generated from each class. For example, if the Lil Dragons class at 3:45pm on Monday and Wednesday has 14 kids, the total income from that class would be $2800 per month.

Assigning instructors a percentage of the income from their respective classes, as discussed in Chapter 3, aligns their interests with the school's. They have a vested interest in maintaining high attendance rates in their classes and recruiting new students.

Furthermore, by knowing the exact value of each class, the school can make informed decisions about scheduling, staffing, and potential expansion. If a class is consistently filled to capacity, it might be worthwhile to consider adding a similar class at a different time.

In conclusion, assigning students to specific time bands is a strategic approach that enhances instruction quality, facilitates resource planning, and helps the school make informed financial decisions. It is a practical strategy that contributes to the overall success of a modern single-style martial arts school.

The Benefits of Strategic Class Addition

In a single-style martial arts school, the addition of new classes should be a strategic decision, guided by a thorough understanding of the school's financials, demographics, and instructional capacity. When a school mindfully curates its class offerings instead of indiscriminately expanding, it reaps several benefits.

Optimized Use of Resources

Each class in the school's schedule represents a commitment of resources: time, space, and instructional expertise. When a class is added strategically, these resources are utilized effectively. The new class serves a specific segment of the student body or addresses a particular training need that is not currently met by existing classes. This ensures that the resources devoted to this class generate maximum value for the school and its students.

Improved Financial Management
Strategic class addition also enhances the school's financial management. When a new class is added, it brings with it predictable revenue, as each class is tied to a specific time band with a known number of students and corresponding fees. This allows the school to accurately forecast the income from this class and adjust its budget and financial plans accordingly.

Enhanced Student Experience

From the students' perspective, the strategic addition of classes contributes to an enhanced training experience. Instead of an overwhelming array of classes with overlapping content, students are offered a carefully curated selection of classes that cater to their age, experience level, and training objectives. This allows them to focus their efforts and progress more effectively in their chosen martial art.

Instructor Engagement and Development

Finally, strategic class addition benefits the school's instructional staff. Instructors have the opportunity to teach new classes, which can be both challenging and rewarding. They can develop their instructional skills and deepen their expertise. Moreover, as the income from each class directly affects their compensation, they have a vested interest in the success of the classes they teach, promoting engagement and dedication.

In conclusion, strategic class addition is a potent tool for a single-style martial arts school. It ensures effective use of resources, improves financial management, enhances student experience, and fosters instructor engagement and development. The result is a school that thrives both operationally and financially, while providing a high-quality training experience to its students.

Chapter 5: Instructor Engagement and Development

- Role and Responsibilities of an Instructor

The role of an instructor in a single-style martial arts school is both diverse and integral. Instructors are not only the conveyors of martial arts techniques but also mentors, motivators, and role models for their students. Their responsibilities extend far beyond simply teaching a class; they contribute significantly to the overall atmosphere, culture, and success of the school.

Teaching and Mentoring

The most apparent responsibility of an instructor is to teach martial arts to their students. They should have a deep mastery of the style they teach and be able to effectively communicate and demonstrate techniques to students of varying age groups and experience levels. A great instructor breaks down complex movements into manageable steps, giving individual feedback and encouragement to help students improve.

Furthermore, instructors often take on a mentoring role. They help students set and achieve their personal goals, be it mastering a specific technique, advancing to the next belt level, or improving their overall fitness. They provide guidance and encouragement, helping students navigate challenges and celebrate achievements.

Creating a Positive Learning Environment Instructors are also responsible for creating a safe, supportive, and motivating learning environment. This involves maintaining discipline and respect in class, ensuring safety guidelines are followed, and promoting a positive, inclusive atmosphere. They help foster a sense of community among students, encouraging teamwork, cooperation, and mutual respect.

Monitoring Student Progress and Class Performance

Instructors play a critical role in monitoring and assessing student progress. They keep track of each student's development, provide constructive feedback, and identify areas for improvement. In a single-style school with assigned time bands, this also involves maintaining class attendance and performance, as it directly impacts their compensation and the financial health of the school.

Promoting the School and Recruiting New Students

Finally, instructors play an essential part in promoting the school and recruiting new students. Their passion for martial arts, teaching skills, and relationship with current students significantly influence the school's reputation and attractiveness to potential students.

In conclusion, the role of an instructor in a single-style martial arts school is multifaceted and crucial. Their responsibilities stretch from teaching and mentoring to creating a positive learning environment, monitoring progress, and promoting the school. As such, their contribution is a key component in the overall success of the school.

- Performance-Based Compensation
In the landscape of a single-style martial arts school, instituting a performance-based compensation system offers an effective means to incentivize instructors and align their efforts with the school's financial success. This approach can boost both the quality of instruction and the financial stability of the school, creating a win-win scenario for all involved. Performance-based compensation means instructors are rewarded based on the financial performance of the classes they teach. In this model, each class or time band is associated with a known revenue based on its capacity and the fees paid by students. A percentage of this revenue is allocated to the instructor as part of their compensation.

This compensation model offers several benefits:

Incentivizing Instructor Performance
Performance-based pay acts as a powerful motivator. When instructors know that the success of their classes directly impacts their income, they have a vested interest in delivering high-quality instruction, retaining current students, and attracting new ones. It encourages them to engage with students beyond the dojo, promoting their classes and the school in the community, which can help boost enrollment.

Aligning Instructor and School Goals
When an instructor's earnings are tied to the revenue of their classes, their financial goals align with those of the school. Instructors become more invested in the school's success, leading to a stronger commitment to their role and a deeper engagement with the school's mission and values.

Promoting Financial Transparency and Fairness

This compensation model also fosters transparency and fairness. Instructors can see how their earnings are calculated and understand the direct link between their efforts and their compensation. It reduces the perception of arbitrary pay decisions, which can enhance job satisfaction and loyalty.

Adapting to School Growth

Finally, a performance-based compensation model can adapt to the growth of the school. As the school attracts more students and adds more classes, instructors have the opportunity to increase their earnings by teaching additional classes or attracting more students to their existing classes.

In conclusion, performance-based compensation provides a strategic tool to motivate and engage instructors, align their efforts with the school's financial success, and promote transparency, fairness, and growth. It is a model worth considering for any modern single-style martial arts school.

Continuous Development and Training for Staff

In the context of a single-style martial arts school, the importance of continuous development and training for instructors cannot be overstated. The journey of martial arts is one of perpetual learning, and this extends equally to both the instructors and the students they teach. The ongoing development of staff can dramatically enhance the quality of instruction, student satisfaction, and overall school success.

At the heart of this process is the recognition that instructors, much like their students, are on a continuous path of growth and improvement. They need regular opportunities to refine their skills, deepen their understanding of the art they teach, and develop their teaching methodologies.

This can be achieved through a variety of methods:

Regular Staff Training Sessions

One effective method is holding regular staff training sessions. These sessions can be used to review and practice techniques, discuss teaching methodologies, share insights about student progress, and address any challenges or issues that have arisen. In this space, instructors can learn from each other, fostering a culture of shared knowledge and continuous improvement.

Professional Development Opportunities

Providing opportunities for professional development, such as workshops, seminars, and certification courses, is another powerful way to enhance staff abilities. These experiences can expose instructors to new ideas, techniques, and approaches that they can bring back to their classes.

Mentorship and Feedback

Creating a culture of feedback and mentorship within the school can also contribute significantly to staff development. More experienced instructors can share their wisdom and experiences with less experienced staff, providing guidance and support. A feedback-rich environment encourages growth, as instructors understand their strengths and areas for improvement.

Encouraging Personal Practice

Encouraging instructors to continue their personal practice and study of martial arts can also enhance their teaching. The depth of their own practice can significantly influence the quality of their instruction, their ability to inspire students, and their capacity to demonstrate and explain complex techniques.

In conclusion, continuous development and training for staff is crucial in a single-style martial arts school. It improves the quality of instruction, fosters a culture of learning and growth, and contributes to the overall success of the school. By investing in their instructors' growth, a school can ensure a high standard of teaching, leading to student satisfaction and retention.

Chapter 6: Marketing and Enrollment

The Advantages of a Single-Style School in Marketing

In the bustling marketplace of martial arts instruction, having a clear, unique selling proposition is crucial for a school to stand out from the competition. Operating as a single-style school presents distinct marketing advantages that can be leveraged to attract new students, retain existing ones, and build a strong brand reputation.

1. Depth of Expertise

One of the most significant advantages of a single-style school is the depth of expertise it offers. By focusing on one style, the school, its instructors, and its curriculum are all geared towards mastering that particular martial art. This commitment to deep, specialized knowledge is highly attractive to potential students seeking comprehensive training in a specific style.

2. Clear Brand Identity

A single-style school has a clear, defined brand identity. The style of martial arts taught becomes a part of the school's identity, making it easily identifiable to potential students. This clarity simplifies marketing messages and makes the school more memorable in the minds of prospective students and their parents.

3. Streamlined Marketing Efforts

With only one style to promote, marketing efforts become more streamlined and efficient. Rather than splitting attention and resources across multiple styles, a single-style school can concentrate its marketing strategies and budget on reaching the target demographic interested in that style. This can result in a more powerful, impactful marketing campaign.

4. Niche Market Appeal

A single-style school appeals to a niche market, which can be a significant advantage in today's highly segmented consumer landscape. Prospective students interested in the specific style the school offers are likely to perceive it as a leading authority in that field, increasing its attractiveness over multi-style schools.

5. Consistency in Instruction

Finally, a single-style school provides consistency in instruction, which is a strong selling point for potential students. Regardless of their age or level of experience, students can expect a cohesive, integrated training experience that builds their skills progressively and systematically.

In conclusion, a single-style martial arts school leverages several marketing advantages: a depth of expertise, a clear brand identity, streamlined marketing efforts, niche market appeal, and consistency in instruction. Each of these advantages can be utilized in marketing strategies to attract and retain students, making a single-style school a strong competitor in the martial arts instruction market.

Additional Revenue Streams: Unlocking Potential Income

In addition to the direct income from regular membership fees, a martial arts school can unlock its potential income by diversifying its revenue streams. By offering additional services and products, the school can maximize its profitability and financial stability. Let's revisit the extra revenue streams you have previously mentioned:

Down Payments from New Signups

Down payments from new signups represent a significant additional revenue stream. With an average of 16 new signups per month, generating an additional $3,200, this practice helps to secure the commitment of new members and contributes to the school's cash flow.

Special Programs

Running specialized programs, like the Women's Only program every six weeks, can draw a distinct demographic of students who may not enroll in regular classes. These programs can be a major attraction, offering an inclusive and safe environment for learning. It has been estimated to generate between $2,500 to $3,000 every six weeks.

Paid-in-Full Memberships

Offering an option for members to pay their annual membership in full at a discounted rate can provide a substantial lump sum to your cash flow. Assuming 20% of your members avail of this, you can gain an additional $4,800.

Summer Camps

Summer camps are a fantastic way to boost revenue during the school vacation periods when regular classes might see a drop in attendance. A two-week summer camp can generate an additional $12,000 per year.

Private and Semi-Private Training

Private and semi-private training sessions offer students personalized attention and customized training plans. This premium service caters to students who are willing to pay extra for these benefits. These sessions can contribute an additional $2,000 to $3,000 every six weeks.

In conclusion, diversifying the school's income sources can significantly enhance its financial health. Not only do these streams provide additional income, but they also serve to increase member engagement, retain students, and attract new members. When planning for additional revenue streams, it is important to align them with the school's primary mission and ensure that they deliver real value to the students.

The Importance of Retaining Existing Students

In the business of martial arts instruction, maintaining a steady roster of dedicated students is as crucial as attracting new ones. In fact, student retention often plays a more significant role in the longevity and success of a martial arts school. Here are some key reasons why retaining existing students is so important:

1. Consistent Revenue Stream

Regular students who attend classes and renew their memberships provide a consistent and predictable revenue stream. This financial stability allows the school to plan for the future, maintain its operations, and invest in improvements.

2. Lower Marketing Costs

Acquiring a new student is typically more expensive than retaining an existing one. The costs of advertising, introductory classes, and other enrollment incentives add up. In contrast, efforts to keep existing students engaged—such as providing high-quality instruction and fostering a welcoming community—are more cost-effective.

3. Higher Lifetime Value

The longer a student stays, the more value they represent in terms of revenue. This lifetime value extends beyond their membership fees. Loyal, long-term students are more likely to purchase additional services, refer friends, and contribute positively to the school community.

4. Stronger Community

Retention contributes to a strong, stable community within the school. Students who train together over time form bonds that can turn a martial arts school into a tight-knit community. This sense of belonging and camaraderie can make the

school a more attractive place for
prospective students.

5. Enhanced Reputation

A high retention rate is a testament to the
quality of instruction and the overall
student experience. It signals to
prospective students that the school is a
place where they can commit, grow, and
achieve their martial arts goals. This
reputation can be a powerful marketing
tool.

In conclusion, focusing on student
retention is a smart strategy for any
martial arts school. It ensures a reliable
revenue stream, lowers marketing costs,
increases the lifetime value of each
student, builds a stronger community, and
enhances the school's reputation. By
prioritizing the satisfaction and success of
current students, a martial arts school can
ensure its long-term sustainability and
growth.

Chapter 7:Managing Your School's Finances

Revenue Potential and Profit Margin Analysis

Managing a martial arts school requires careful handling of finances. Recognizing the various sources of income, understanding the expenditures, and analyzing profit margins are critical components to ensure the financial health and growth of your institution. Here, we revisit your revenue potential and assess your profit margins:

Revenue Potential

As detailed earlier, your martial arts school has significant revenue potential from a variety of sources. This includes:

- Membership fees for Lil Dragons, Juniors, BBT, and Teens classes with a total potential of $32,400 per month.

- Adult classes offering different programs with a potential of $12,000 to $16,000 per month.

- Additional revenue streams including down payments, specialized programs, summer camps, and private training which can contribute significant sums at various intervals.

When added together, your martial arts school has a substantial monthly revenue potential. This income can serve as the lifeblood of your school, fueling everything from payroll to rent, utilities, and reinvestment in the business.

Profit Margin Analysis

To understand the profitability of your school, you need to subtract your expenses from your total revenue. Let's take a look at potential costs:

- **Rent**: Rent is likely to be one of your biggest monthly expenses. Ideally, it should be less than 15-20% of your gross income.

- **Salaries**: The wages for your instructors and any administrative or cleaning staff will constitute a major portion of your expenses. A performance-based compensation system can help manage these costs effectively.

- **Utilities and Maintenance**: Costs for utilities such as electricity, water, and internet, along with regular maintenance, should be factored into your monthly expenses.

- **Marketing and Advertising**: These costs can fluctuate based on your strategies and needs. A focus on retention can help minimize these expenses.

- **Equipment and Supplies**: Regular replacements or upgrades of training equipment, purchasing supplies for cleaning, and maintaining your premises are additional costs to consider.

Once you have a clear understanding of your total monthly expenses, subtract them from your total monthly income to ascertain your profit. The result is your profit margin, which serves as a key indicator of your school's financial health. A high profit margin signifies a highly profitable and efficient operation.

It's essential to consistently review and adjust your financial strategies as necessary, optimizing your revenue streams and controlling expenses. Managing your school's finances effectively is crucial for long-term stability, growth, and success.

Understanding the Breakdown of Expenses

Running a martial arts school is rewarding, but it also comes with various expenses. Understanding these costs is essential to managing your school's budget effectively and ensuring financial stability.

Let's delve into the major categories of expenditures:

1. Rent and Utilities: This includes the cost of renting your school's premises and the costs of utilities like electricity, water, heating, and internet. Rent is generally one of the most significant monthly costs, and it's advisable to keep it below 15-20% of your gross income. Utilities are a necessary expenditure for running your classes and maintaining a comfortable environment for your students.

2. Salaries and Wages: Paying your instructors and any administrative or cleaning staff constitutes a substantial portion of your expenses. The salaries should be balanced against the revenue they help generate. Implementing a performance-based compensation system can be an effective way to manage this cost.

3. Equipment and Supplies: Regular replacement or upgrading of training equipment, and the purchasing of cleaning supplies and uniforms, are additional costs to factor in. While these expenses contribute to the quality of your program, it's important to find a balance between quality and cost-efficiency.

4. Marketing and Advertising: The cost of marketing your school to attract new students can be significant. This can include online advertising, printing brochures, hosting open houses, or offering trial classes. However, effective student retention strategies can help reduce the need for constant and costly advertising.

5. Administrative Costs: These are the costs associated with running the business side of your school, such as insurance, licensing fees, software for managing student registrations and billing, and professional services like accounting or legal advice.

6. Maintenance: The cost of regular maintenance of your premises, including cleaning and minor repairs, contributes to the overall student experience and is an essential part of your expenses.

Understanding these costs provides a clearer picture of where your money is going each month. It can help you identify areas where you might reduce costs or increase efficiency. By carefully managing these expenses against your revenue, you can ensure the financial health and sustainability of your martial arts school.

Aligning Costs and Revenue for Financial Success

Financial success in running a martial arts school involves aligning costs and revenue effectively. It's not just about increasing revenue; it's equally important to manage and control expenses. Here are key strategies to align your costs and revenue for financial success:

Understand Your Costs: A clear understanding of your costs is the first step in managing them effectively. As we discussed earlier, costs for a martial arts school can range from rent and salaries to marketing, equipment, administrative costs, and maintenance. Regularly review these costs and identify any trends or areas where you might be able to reduce expenses without sacrificing the quality of your programs.

Boost Your Revenue Streams: Look for ways to maximize your revenue. This can involve expanding your existing programs, offering specialized classes, or implementing additional revenue streams such as private training sessions or summer camps. Remember, the value proposition should always be clear to your students; they should understand what they're paying for and see the benefits.

Balance Quality and Cost: While it's essential to provide high-quality training and a positive experience for your students, you should also keep costs in mind. Investing in top-quality equipment, for instance, is necessary, but regular maintenance can extend its life and delay replacement costs. Similarly, a well-maintained, clean school environment contributes to student satisfaction and retention, minimizing marketing costs for new student acquisition.

Implement Performance-Based Compensation: As discussed earlier, tying instructor compensation to performance and the revenue they help generate can create a vested interest in the school's success. This can increase motivation, retention, and overall quality of instruction, enhancing student satisfaction and thereby boosting your revenue.

Prioritize Student Retention: Retaining existing students is more cost-effective than constantly acquiring new ones. By focusing on providing excellent instruction and a well-structured program, you can enhance student satisfaction and increase retention rates, maintaining a steady stream of revenue.

Plan for Unexpected Expenses: It's wise to set aside a portion of your revenue to cover unexpected expenses, whether it's equipment that needs replacing or an unexpected increase in rent or utilities. Having a buffer can help you navigate these unexpected costs without compromising your school's financial health.

Remember, financial success doesn't come overnight. It requires careful planning, consistent management, and a constant eye on the bottom line. However, with careful alignment of costs and revenue, your martial arts school can achieve financial stability and success.

Chapter 7:The Power of a Rotating Curriculum

The Power of a Rotating Curriculum: Scalability and Efficiency in Teaching

The modern martial arts school's success hinges upon its ability to provide a comprehensive, enriching, and engaging training experience. One proven way to achieve this is through the implementation of a rotating curriculum.

A rotating curriculum is an innovative approach to teaching martial arts that divides the curriculum into smaller, manageable parts, often referred to as cycles or modules. These modules are then taught in rotation throughout the year. This methodology provides both scalability and efficiency in teaching, enabling martial arts schools to meet the diverse needs of their students while maximizing resources.

Here's a deeper look at how a rotating curriculum can power the success of your martial arts school:

Scalability: In the context of a martial arts school, scalability refers to the ability to grow or expand the school's operations and student base without a significant increase in resources or decrease in the quality of instruction. A rotating curriculum allows for this scalability. It provides a structured framework that can be implemented regardless of the class size or skill level, ensuring all students receive comprehensive training. As the school grows and more students enroll, the rotating curriculum can be maintained without requiring a proportional increase in resources.

Efficiency: A rotating curriculum promotes teaching efficiency by providing a clear, structured roadmap for instruction. With a set schedule of modules, instructors can plan lessons well in advance and ensure each class is productive and engaging. Moreover, this approach eliminates the need to tailor individual lesson plans for different skill levels. Instead, each module can be taught with slight adaptations to cater to the varying skill levels within a class, from beginners to advanced students.

Consistency: With a rotating curriculum, every student, regardless of when they join, receives the same comprehensive training over a given period. This eliminates gaps in knowledge and skills that can arise when students join at different times and ensures a consistent training experience.

Flexibility: Despite its structured nature, a rotating curriculum offers flexibility. Each module can be revised, updated, or swapped out to keep the curriculum current and engaging. This can be particularly beneficial in a single-style school, where keeping the curriculum dynamic and exciting can enhance student retention.

Student Progression: A rotating curriculum provides clear progression paths for students. They know what to expect from each module and what skills they need to master before moving on to the next one. This clarity can boost motivation and engagement, contributing to improved student retention.

In sum, a rotating curriculum offers a powerful framework for a single-style martial arts school. It provides scalability, teaching efficiency, and a consistent, flexible, and clear path for student progression, which are key ingredients in the recipe for a successful, modern martial arts school.

Designing and Implementing a Rotating Curriculum

Designing and implementing a rotating curriculum in a single-style martial arts school is an essential step to achieve the objectives of efficient, scalable, and effective teaching. It requires careful planning, organization, and a thorough understanding of the martial art being taught. The following points provide a roadmap for creating and integrating a rotating curriculum into your school's system:

Understanding the Core Concepts

Before you begin designing the curriculum, it's vital to have a deep understanding of the martial art style you're teaching. You should be familiar with the key techniques, forms, theories, and principles of the style. This understanding will allow you to break down the larger discipline into teachable, comprehensive modules.

Defining Modules

Based on the comprehensive understanding of your martial art, divide the style into separate modules. A module can be centered around a specific set of techniques, a principle, a form, or any other relevant aspect. Ensure each module is manageable in size, has specific learning objectives, and aligns with the overall progression of the style.

Scheduling the Rotation

Once the modules are defined, schedule them in a logical rotation. The order should take into consideration the difficulty level, the progressive development of skills, and the optimal learning paths for students. For instance, a module on basic techniques might precede a module on advanced forms that incorporate these techniques.

Balancing Consistency and Variation

While a rotating curriculum provides a consistent framework, it's important to balance consistency with variation to keep students engaged. Ensure that the modules are varied enough to prevent the curriculum from becoming repetitive and stale, but consistent enough to reinforce learning and progression.

Implementing and Testing

Upon designing the curriculum and scheduling the rotation, implement it in your classes. It may be beneficial to start on a smaller scale, perhaps with one age group or experience level, to test the effectiveness of the curriculum. Gather feedback from both instructors and students to identify areas for improvement.

Review and Revise

Regularly review the curriculum to ensure it's meeting its goals. Look for areas where students consistently struggle or excel and adjust the curriculum accordingly. This could involve changing the order of modules, adding new ones, or removing those that don't contribute to students' development. Regular revision keeps the curriculum dynamic and relevant.

Designing and implementing a rotating curriculum is a significant undertaking, but it is a worthwhile investment. By providing a structured, scalable, and efficient approach to teaching, a rotating curriculum can greatly enhance the student experience and the overall success of your single-style martial arts school.

Summarizing:

Potential revenue of the school was:

- Lil Dragons: $8,400/month
- Juniors: $12,000/month
- Advanced Juniors (BBT): $6,000/month
- Teens: $6,000/month
- Adults: $12,000 - $16,000/month
- Additional Revenue: $2,500 - $3,000 (6 Week Women's only, every 6 weeks), $4,800 (Paid in Full), $2,000 - $3,000 (Semi-private sessions, every 6 weeks), $12,000 (Summer camp), and Private Training income.

For simplicity, let's consider an average scenario where adult classes bring in $14,000/month and the additional revenue is $3,000 for women's classes and $2,500 for semi-private sessions every six weeks. This makes the total gross monthly revenue of the school:

$8,400 (Lil Dragons) + $12,000 (Juniors) + $6,000 (BBT) + $6,000 (Teens) + $14,000 (Adults) + [($3,000 + $4,800 +

$2,500 + $12,000)/6] (Additional Revenue) = $52,300

Now, let's look at the main categories of expenses. For simplicity, we'll estimate them as a percentage of gross revenue:

- Rent: 10-15% of gross revenue
- Wages and Salaries: 20-30% of gross revenue
- Utilities and Maintenance: We'll estimate this as 5% of gross revenue
- Marketing and Advertising: 7-8% of gross revenue
- Insurance and Licenses: These can vary greatly, but we'll estimate 3% of gross revenue for this example
- Supplies and Equipment: These costs will also vary, but we'll estimate 5% of gross revenue

Totaling these percentages, we estimate expenses to be around 50-66% of gross revenue. This leaves us with a gross profit margin of 34-50%.

For the $52,300 monthly revenue, the estimated monthly profit before taxes would be $17,782 - $26,150. This demonstrates a healthy profit margin for the school. However, it's important to note that these are rough estimates. Actual costs can vary based on many factors including the local market, the specific agreements with staff, and the efficiency of the school's operations.

It's also worth noting that this profit margin will vary over time, particularly as the school grows and adds more classes and students. For a martial arts school, growth often means higher revenue, but it also means higher costs. Effective management of both revenue and costs is crucial for maintaining a healthy profit margin.

Kids can only train 1 or 2 times per week **1x per week is $150 per month ($37.5 per class)** **2x per week is $200 per month ($25 per class)**	**Price includes: shirt, pants, belt, gloves and shin-pads)** **We do not change any other fees for ranking and belts**
Lil Dragons **5-7 y/o** **30 min classes** **Capacity 14 ($2,800/ month each band)**	
M/W 3:45pm	
M/W 5:45pm	
T/TH 4:45pm	
Total based on capacity:	$8,400 per month
Juniors **8-12 y/o** **45 min classes** **Capacity 20 ($4,000/ month each band)**	
M/W 4:15pm	
M/W 6:15pm	
T/TH 4:00pm	
Total based on capacity:	$12,000 per month
BBT **Advanced juniors** **45 min classes** **Capacity 30 ($6,000/ month each band)**	$6,000 per month
T/Th 5:15 pm	

Teens **12-17 y/o** **45 min classes** **Capacity 30 ($6,000/** **month each band)**	$6,000 per month
M/W 7:00pm	
Total income potential based on current schedule: Based only on kids and teens	$32,400 per month
ADULT PROGRAMS **1 x per week $150/month** **2x per week $200/month** **Unlimited $250/month**	Capacity 60/80 students divided among all classes Most students are on a 2x per week Monthly potential $12,000/16,000
M/W 5:00pm Krav Maga	
T/Th 7:00pm Krav Maga	
T/Th 12:00pm Krav Maga	
Sat 9:15am Krav Maga	
T/Th 6:00pm FightLab/ GroundLab	
Additional revenue:	
Down-payments from new signups: 16 monthly $3,200	6 Week Women's only (done every 6 weeks) $2,500 to $3,000

Paid in full: 4 or 20% $4,800	Summer camp 2 weeks per year at $6,000 per week ($12,000 total
Private training misc income	Semi-private sessions $2,000 to $3,000 every 6 weeks

Printed in Great Britain
by Amazon

38673758R00046